THE LIFE CYCLE OF A POLAR BEAR

Written by Catriona Clarke

CONTENTS

Arctic habitat	2
New life	8
Early life	18
Growing up	32
Adulthood	38
Glossary	44
Index	45
The life cycle of a polar bear	46

Collins

ARCTIC HABITAT

Polar bears are big, powerful white bears. They may look cuddly, but they are fierce **predators**. In fact, they are the biggest of all land predators.

Polar bears live in the Arctic. This is where they grow up, hunt for food, and have babies of their own. Let's find out more about the life of a polar bear and how they manage to survive in the frozen north.

Male polar bears are much bigger than the females.

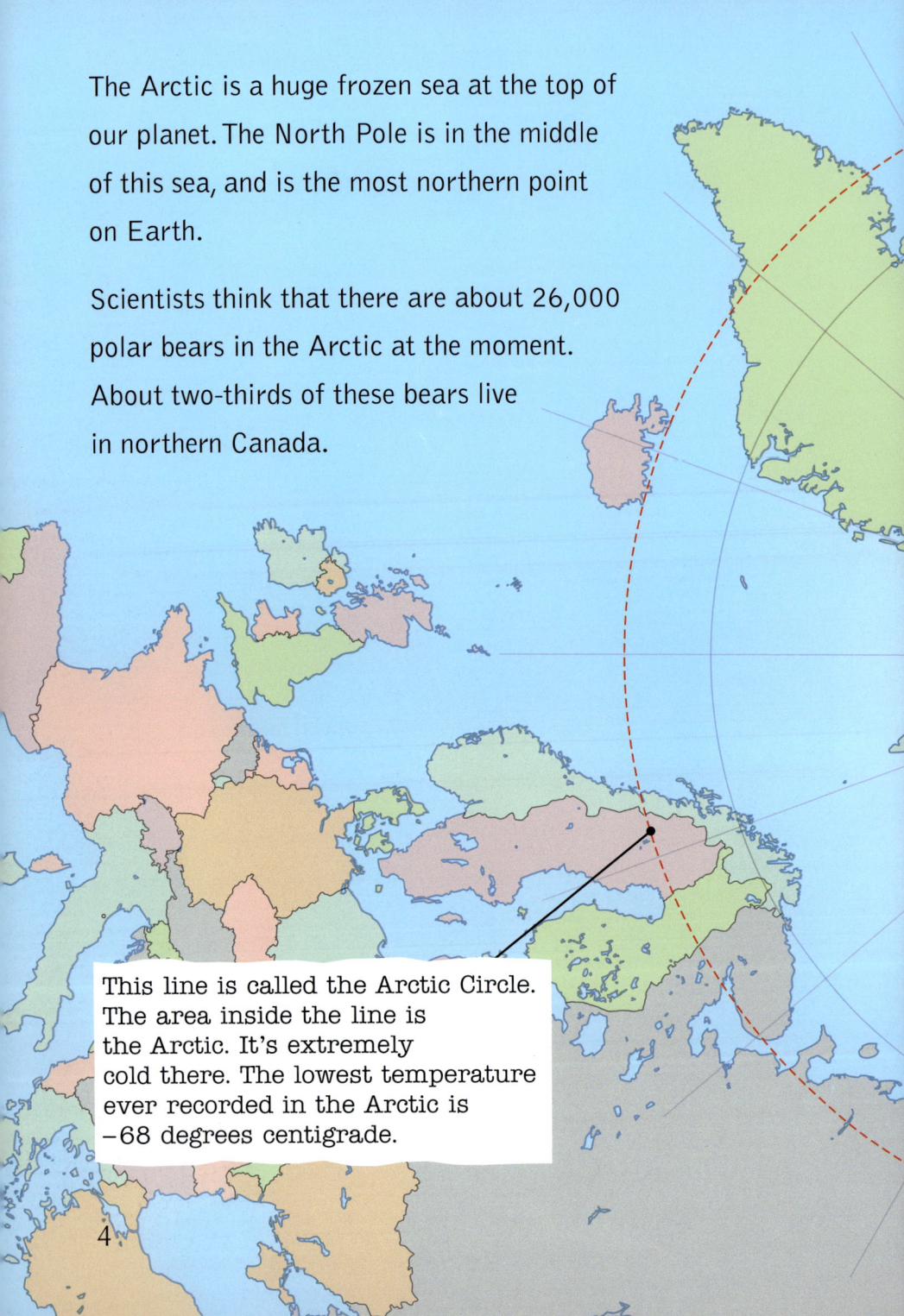

The Arctic is a huge frozen sea at the top of our planet. The North Pole is in the middle of this sea, and is the most northern point on Earth.

Scientists think that there are about 26,000 polar bears in the Arctic at the moment. About two-thirds of these bears live in northern Canada.

This line is called the Arctic Circle. The area inside the line is the Arctic. It's extremely cold there. The lowest temperature ever recorded in the Arctic is −68 degrees centigrade.

DID YOU KNOW?

In the Arctic summertime, it doesn't get dark at night. In winter, the sun doesn't come out during the day.

The frozen ocean water of the Arctic is called sea ice. Some of the ice is so thick that it stays frozen all year round, but thinner ice melts in summertime. This type of sea ice is called annual ice.

Annual ice is where polar bears live for most of the year. It's a difficult **environment** for animals to survive in, but it's perfect for the polar bear. Animals living above and below the sea ice provide all the food the bear needs.

This bear is walking on annual ice in the Svalbard area of Norway.

NEW LIFE

In springtime, it gets warmer in the Arctic and the sea ice starts to melt. This is when adult male polar bears start searching for females. It isn't easy. A male bear may travel for hundreds of miles before he finds a female ready for mating.

The male finds the tracks of a female and follows them until he catches up with her. This can take days. If another male is nearby, the two bears will fight.

The bigger bear throws the other bear onto its back and grabs its throat. The smaller bear lies still until the bigger bear lets go. Then the smaller bear slinks away.

FACT
Adult male bears often have broken teeth and scars on their heads and necks from fighting other bears.

The male and the female stay together for a week or two and mate several times. Then they go their separate ways. The male bear will have nothing to do with the mother and the cubs she will have in eight months' time.

In summer, the sea ice is nearly gone. This makes hunting more difficult for polar bears because the fish and seals they eat live under the sea ice. The pregnant female has to find as much food as she can to prepare for winter.

FACT

A pregnant bear needs to gain at least 100 kilograms of fat. That's the same weight as 100 roast chickens! The bear needs to store fat, as she won't have any food to eat when she enters her den.

LEAVING THE ICE

The sea ice starts to form again in autumn. This is when pregnant females head towards land to look for the perfect safe place to build their den. They need to find somewhere far enough away from where male bears are hunting, but close enough to the sea ice so that the journey back in springtime won't be too long. The male bears stay out on the sea ice through the winter.

A pregnant female will spend a few days finding the perfect place to build her den. She looks for banks of snow that have been formed by the wind. She pokes and prods the snow and digs small holes to test it. Hard, tightly packed snow is best.

When the bear has found the right spot, she begins to dig. The den will be her home for the next four months. She will rest in this sheltered, safe space until her cubs are born.

13

INSIDE THE DEN

In winter, it's dark and stormy outside, but it's warm inside the den. The temperature can be 20 degrees centigrade warmer than it is outside.

The entrance tunnel is long and narrow. It is barely wide enough for the mother bear to fit through.

Sometimes there's a hole so that fresh air can enter the den.

The main **chamber** is higher than the entrance tunnel to keep in warmer air.

The chamber is just big enough for the mother bear and her cubs.

A few weeks after the bear enters the den, her cubs are born. Polar bears usually give birth to twins. The newborn cubs' eyes are closed and their fur is almost invisible. Their tiny paws are tipped with sharp claws.

The tiny cubs feed on the mother's milk. The milk is very fatty and high in **protein**, which helps the cubs to grow quickly. The mother and cubs stay inside the den for three months while the cubs grow bigger and stronger.

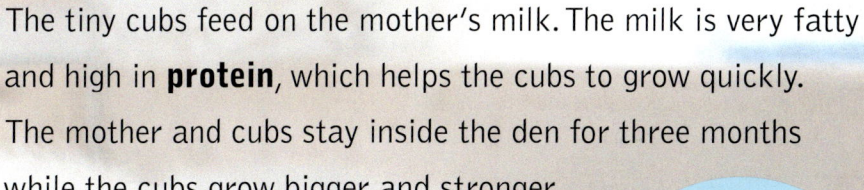

FACT
Polar bears are tiny when they are born. They are about the same size as a guinea pig.

These cubs were born in **captivity**.

EARLY LIFE

When the cubs are three months old, it's time to leave the den as the mother needs to eat. By now, it's springtime again. The mother pushes upwards to break through the den's roof. She sticks out her nose and sniffs the air to check for any danger. If it seems safe, she clambers out of the den and the cubs follow her. This is the first time the polar bear cubs will have seen the outside world.

These cubs are feeding on their mother's milk.

The family will stay near to the den for a few days. The cubs stay very close to their mother at first, while they get used to the strange sights, sounds and smells. They spend a lot of time resting and feeding.

The mother is very hungry after eight months without food, but she must wait until the cubs are strong enough before heading to the sea ice.

Heading back to the sea ice is difficult for the cubs after spending three months inside their small den. It's still very cold, and the cubs tire easily. Sometimes they climb onto the mother's back so she can carry them.

The journey is dangerous too. The mother bear must look out for adult males who might try to attack and eat her cubs.

The family stops to rest regularly and the cubs feed on their mother's milk. By the time they reach the sea ice, the mother is desperate for food. It's time to hunt.

> **DID YOU KNOW?**
> A mother bear and her cubs can run faster than an adult male.

THE ARCTIC FOOD CHAIN

Seals and beluga whales eat fish living underneath the sea ice. Because the seals need to come up to the surface of the water to breathe, they are easy for polar bears to catch. Beluga whales also need to come up for air, but luckily for them, they are much more difficult for the bears to catch. This is partly because of their size and also, unlike seals, they never leave the water.

Beluga whales are one of the smallest types of whale.

Polar bears don't have to worry about any other animal trying to eat them. They are at the top of the Arctic food chain.

seals

polar bears

large fish, such as cod

small fish

plankton

23

Polar bears are expert hunters by the time they are adults. Their favourite animal to eat is the ringed seal.

The bears need to eat as much as possible now, because sea ice is the best hunting ground. When the sea ice **retreats** in summertime, there will be less food available.

This ringed seal is checking if it is safe to leave the water.

In springtime, there are lots of seal pups in the Arctic. They are easier to catch than adult seals because they're smaller and unaware of the danger from predators. Their bodies are very fatty, giving the bears lots of energy.

FACT
Seals have very strong, fishy breath! Polar bears can sniff the air and tell if a seal was there recently.

STALKING SEALS

When a polar bear smells or sees a ringed seal basking on the ice, it stalks the seal.

1 The bear stops moving the moment it sees the seal.

2 The bear lowers its head and crouches down, walking slowly towards its **prey**.

3 When the bear is a few metres away, it **charges** while the seal scrambles to escape.

4 The bear grabs the seal by the head, and drags it away from the hole in case it tries to escape.

WATCH AND LEARN

The cubs follow their mother closely as she hunts, watching everything she does. They learn to sniff in the same places she does to check for nearby prey.

FACT
A polar bear lying down next to a seal's breathing hole may look like it's resting, but it's probably waiting for a seal's head to pop out of the water.

The cubs usually sit quietly while the mother hunts, but sometimes they get bored. Then they start to play, chasing each other across the ice. The mother gets annoyed if the cubs scare the seals away.

FACT
Polar bear cubs enjoy chasing each other, play-fighting and rolling down icy slopes. In summer, they like to run through shallow pools of water on the ice.

The cubs will eventually learn to watch their mother carefully. It's very important that they learn how to hunt, even though they won't need to do it themselves until they are 18 months old. When they first try hunting, they hardly ever catch anything because they're not big or strong enough.

The cubs stay with their mother until they are about two and a half years old. The cubs need to grow big enough to be able to hunt well. By the time they are two years old, male cubs are often bigger than their mothers.

The young bears can now hunt quite successfully, but while they are still feeding on their mother's milk, they don't actually need to. They will only start hunting for all their food when they leave their mother.

The mother is now ready to mate again and adult males are searching for females once more. When the male arrives, he or the mother will chase the cubs away. The cubs probably won't see their mother again.

GROWING UP

Polar bears live on their own for most of the time, so the young bears must now survive alone. At this stage of their life, they are known as sub-adults.

Older, bigger bears often steal their food. The younger bear won't bother fighting the older bear, because it would get badly injured. This is why sub-adults often have to make do with leftover food.

ICE SPECIALISTS

Life is hard for young polar bears, but they are perfectly adapted to their environment.

A long neck and head mean that the bear can stick its head into holes in the ice without getting stuck.

The bear has a thick layer of **blubber** to keep it warm.

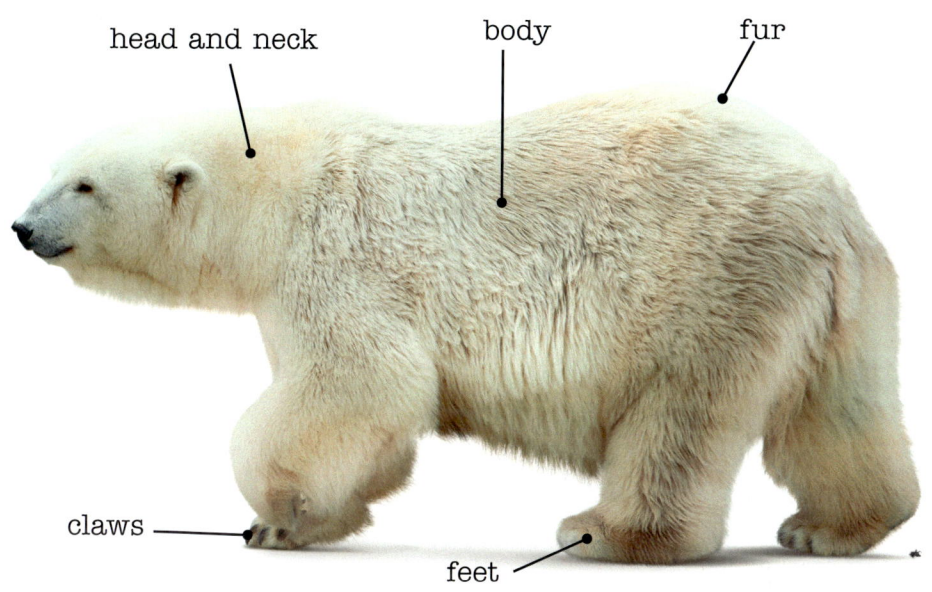

head and neck

body

fur

claws

feet

The thick fur is not actually white. The hairs are see-through and **reflect** light, so that the bear looks white amongst the ice and snow.

Huge feet are good for swimming. They also spread the bear's weight so it can walk on thin ice.

PAWS AND CLAWS

A polar bear's paws are almost as big as its head. The pads are covered in tiny bumps that help the bear walk across the slippery ice. The short claws are also useful for gripping the ice, and are strong enough to dig through ice too.

The bear uses its huge paws to paddle through the water. The front paws are slightly webbed to make this easier. The back paws act like a rudder on a boat, helping the bear to change direction in the water.

DID YOU KNOW?

Scientists watched one female polar bear swimming non-stop for nine days in the Beaufort Sea, north of Alaska. The bear was swimming from the sea ice to the land. This is the longest polar bear swim ever recorded.

STAYING COOL

Polar bears spend a lot of their time plodding across the ice quite slowly. This is so that they don't get too hot. Their thick fur and blubber make it easy for them to overheat.

> **DID YOU KNOW?**
> A polar bear can run as fast as a horse, but it gets too hot and has to stop after a few minutes.

On warm summer days, polar bears go for a swim to cool off. They also sprawl on the ice. They lie on their tummies with their feet spread out, or on their backs with their feet in the air, like this young male. This lowers their body temperature.

ADULTHOOD

Polar bears reach adulthood when they are between four and six years old. Adult males are up to two and a half metres long, and usually weigh from 350 to 600 kilograms. The females are smaller and less than half the weight of the males.

FACT
The heaviest polar bear ever recorded weighed 1,000 kilograms – the same as a small car.

1,000 kilograms

1,000 kilograms

Polar bears are very clean animals. They wash for about 15 minutes after eating. In summer, they wash in pools of water on the ice. In winter, the bears roll around in the snow.

THE CIRCLE OF LIFE

Eventually, adult polar bears are ready to look for a mate. The male bears have to wait until they are eight to ten years old before they are big and strong enough to compete with other males and mate with a female. Once spring comes along, the life cycle begins again.

Most polar bears live between 15 and 20 years, but some live for 30 years or more.

PEOPLE AND BEARS

Every year, thousands of people visit the Arctic to get a chance to see polar bears in the wild. The town of Churchill, Manitoba in Canada is known as the polar bear capital of the world. In the autumn, polar bears pass through this town on their way to the sea ice.

These tourists were able to get very close to the bears without any danger.

THE FUTURE

Polar bears are very successful predators, but they need the sea ice to be able to hunt. Sadly, **global warming** means that the sea ice is breaking up earlier in the year.

This means that many polar bears don't have access to the food they need. Some bears starve during the long winter, and fewer cubs are being born. Scientists predict that two-thirds of the world's polar bears will be gone by the end of this century if nothing changes.

People can help slow down global warming by creating less pollution. There is still time to save the polar bear so that this amazing animal will still be here for hundreds of years to come.

GLOSSARY

blubber   a thick layer of fat under the skin of polar bears and other animals that live in cold waters; it keeps the animals warm

captivity   when an animal is not living in the wild

chamber   an enclosed space

charges   runs quickly towards something

environment   the place where an animal lives

global warming the gradual increase in our planet's temperature, which is caused by pollution

plankton   tiny plant and animal life found in the sea

predators   animals that eat other animals

prey   the animals hunted and eaten by a predator

protein   a type of food that animals need to grow and stay healthy

reflect   throw back light

retreats   moves back

INDEX

adults 8, 21, 24–25, 31, 38, 40

annual ice 6–7

Arctic 2, 4–5, 6, 8, 22–23, 25, 41

babies 2

beluga whale 22

Canada 4, 41

claws 16, 33, 34

cubs 10, 12–21, 28–31, 42

den 10, 12–20, 46

female polar bears 8, 10, 12, 31, 35, 38, 40

food 2, 7, 10, 19, 21–24, 30, 32, 42

food chain 22–23

global warming 42–43

hunting 10, 12, 24, 29–30

male polar bears 3, 8, 10, 12, 21, 30–31, 37–38, 40

mate / mating 8, 10, 31, 40, 47

milk 17, 21, 30

North Pole 4

paws 16, 34–35

pollution 43

predators 2, 25, 42

sea ice 6–8, 10, 12, 19–22, 24, 35, 41–42, 46

seals 10, 22–27, 29

snow 12, 33, 39

sub-adults 32

45

THE LIFE CYCLE OF A POLAR BEAR

2 leaving den to walk to sea ice with mother

1 bear cub

7 pregnant female makes den

3 learning to sniff air, playing

4 left alone

6 finding a mate

5 hunting/feeding

47

Ideas for reading

Written by Clare Dowdall, PhD
Lecturer and Primary Literacy Consultant

Reading objectives:
- retrieve and record information from non-fiction
- ask questions to improve understanding
- identify main ideas drawn from more than one paragraph and summarise ideas

Spoken language objectives:
- participate in discussions, presentations, performances, role play, improvisations and debates

Curriculum links: Science – Living things and their habitats

Resources: ICT, paper and pens.

Build a context for reading
- Ask children to suggest what a life cycle is, and to recount the stages in their own life cycle.
- Explain that you will be reading about the life cycle of a polar bear. Start to gather known facts using a spider diagram.
- Look at the cover and read the blurb together. Help children raise questions about the polar bear's life cycle and survival, based on their known facts.

Understand and apply reading strategies
- Turn to the contents. Discuss how the chapter headings work to organise the information as a life cycle.
- Read pp2–3 aloud. Ask children to explain what a predator is. Model using the glossary to check the meaning of the word *predator*.
- Ask a volunteer to read pp4–5. Look at the map together. Help children to locate Britain and Canada, and discuss what the habitat in the Arctic is like.